The Story of

S T E R L I N G

THUMB-NAIL HISTORICAL AND
USEFUL FACTS ABOUT THE CRAFT
"WHERE ART AND INDUSTRY MEET"

published by

THE STERLING SILVERSMITHS GUILD OF AMERICA
551 Fifth Avenue   **New York, N. Y.**

Price Fifty Cents

YOUR STERLING AND YOU

Fine Sterling carries with it the same unquestioned authority as other authentic works of art . . . the inescapable authority of the genuine. Reproductions may frequently be mistaken for the original . . . but the genuine carries an assurance that is rarely confused with its imitators. This is true of people; of books; of paintings; of furniture; of gems; in an especial degree, it is true of silver. And this *authority of the genuine* contributes to the people whose lives it touches daily a sense of permanence, of continuity that can come from no other source. It is more than pride of possession. It is a reflection of the quality of the thing itself. A simple dinner served with things of permanent beauty becomes memorable. And coffee poured from a slender shining pot of silver is a libation to the guest under the roof-tree. Too much importance, you say, to attach to material possessions? But they are part of the ritual of daily life. And to dignify them with permanence and beauty is to dignify daily life itself.

Jean Parker

Cellini in his workshop

BENVENUTO CELLINI
1500-1571

$\mathcal{S}ilver$... THE AGELESS METAL

Silver has held an intriguing fascination for man from the early dawn of history. Its glorious beauty, durability and workability ranked it in the beginning as one of earth's most precious metals. Its use in the making of articles of tableware goes back as far as we can trace the history of civilization itself.

*Vase about
1300 B. C.*

Excavations in Egypt at Beni Hassam have brought to light carefully drawn documents in the form of decorations cut in stone, depicting the craft of silversmithing, and archaeologists date these about 2,500 years B.C. Actual pieces of wrought silver, such as bowls and vases, that date back as far as 1,900 B.C., can be found in the museums of the world. The books of the Old Testament speak of the silversmith and his craft, and silver, the metal, is referred to time and again. In "Genesis" we read of "Abram who was rich in gold, in silver and in cattle," while in "Acts" we learn of "Demetrius, a silversmith, who made silver shrines for Diana."

*Silver Jug from
Cypress about 700
to 500 B. C.*

Down through the ages this romantic metal has been honored and valued by every nation that has left its mark on the pages of history. Small wonder it has been crowned with the title it so regally wears—the "Queen of Metals."

Evidence of the far-reaching imaginative effect of silver on all races and classes of men throughout the world is to be found in the very words and common phrases that have been incorporated into our everyday speech. We are all familiar with such expressions as "silvery moonlight," "silvery music," "silver tongued orator," "The cloud with its silver lining," etc. The counterpart of these, and like silvery phrases in English, are found in every tongue. In every land the thought of shining silver has always been employed to signify wealth, prosperity, purity, happiness, temporal and spiritual well-being.

*Grecian Drinking
Cup 3rd Century
B. C.*

Grecian Ladle about 300 B. C.

We turn to Homer, the Greek poet, and there we find reference to "gold and silver vessels;" "silver wine cups are given as rewards;" and "the wine bowl of silver stands in the entrance hall on a tripod." Centuries later, in the glory that was Rome, Horace writes of "homes that gleamed with silver;" Cicero of "wrought and stamped silver;" and Pliny describes "suppers served on pure and antique silver." All through the classics countless references are made to cups, platters, dishes and other tableware "wrought in gleaming silver."

Then came the Goths and their destruction of civilization. Art was swept away and much of the world's artistic treasure of wrought gold and silver was destroyed. For almost a thousand years the Light of Civilization flickered, and then, in the XIV Century, in Italy, there came the Renaissance—the re-birth of art and culture—which spread to France and thence to England. Silver tableware again graced the tables of cultured people and the art of silversmithing has flourished ever since, employing the finest artist-craftsmen in each generation.

The silver which we have been speaking of is *Solid Silver*. Down through the ages it has always been Solid Silver. There was no such thing as an imitation until about 200 years ago, and there never has been anything "just as good." Throughout the history of silver the quality of the metal has been most important. *Pure* metallic silver is too soft for practical use—a spoon of unalloyed pure silver, for example, would bend and finally break in ordinary use. To overcome this *ductility* of the metal, a small portion of copper is added, or alloyed, to the pure silver before the craftsman begins to work it. But only 75 parts of copper need be added to every 925 parts of pure silver. Silver of this quality is known as STERLING.

Etruscan Toilet Box 400 B. C.

The word "Sterling" is believed to be a contraction of the word "Easterlings," which was the name of a band of traders of the twelfth century, during the reign of Richard I.

They came from the eastern part of Germany and in trading with the English offered "tokens" (pieces of metal corresponding to coins) in exchange for goods. These tokens were made of a silver alloy which was noted for its purity and the uniform high standard of 925/1000 fine, and were adopted by the English for use in commerce.

The Sterling standard has, for centuries, been recognized as the ideal quality for all purposes, and it is the standard used by reliable silversmiths to-day. Since 1907 the mark "Sterling" has had the protection of United States law; all silver stamped "Sterling" *must* contain 925 parts of pure silver in every 1000 parts of metal.

Roman Spoon
4th Century

Therefore, always look for the stamp "Sterling" when purchasing silver tableware for this is your protection in obtaining genuine Solid Silver—the same high quality of metal all the way through each piece.

The ancients were not wrong in seeking a beautiful pure metal for their tableware. There is every reason why one's knives, forks and spoons should be Sterling. What touches one more personally than table silver—the utensils with which food is eaten? There is no cleaner, more sanitary, nor more beautiful metal than silver. There is nothing to wear off so that it will lose its loveliness.

In fine silver has been written the history of the ages— the culture and artistic tastes of past generations. It lasts after all else has gone. And the fine Sterling Silver Tableware you buy to-day will not only glorify your own home but will become a lasting symbol to future generations of your good taste and love for worthwhile possessions.

German Cup
17th Century

Salt Cellar by
Benvenuto Cellini.
Made in 1530

9

PAUL REVERE

1735-1818

10

$\mathscr{America's}$ HERITAGE

Of all the periods in the world's history of Silver, one of the most fascinating is that which covers early America. The collections of Colonial Silver in the Metropolitan Museum of Art in New York, in the Museum of Fine Arts in Boston and in other leading museums of the country display a grace in line and a perfection in proportion of which any age and nation might well be proud.

Among the settlers of this country was a group of remarkable silversmiths, as is accepted and proven by the high standard of their workmanship. We cannot escape, too, that there must have been a keen and wide appreciation for fine silver among our forefathers to have supported so many silversmiths, for, in Colonial newspapers and archives of various sorts, one finds that literally hundreds of silversmiths flourished in the Colonies.

Left: Earliest known Colonial Spoon. Made by Hull (1624-83)

Right: Spoon by Coney (1655-1722)

The earliest mentioned silversmith in America is one Thomas Howard whose presence in Jamestown is recorded as of 1620 in the register of the Virginia Company. John Mansfield, silversmith, was working in Charlestown, Massachusetts, in 1634. Early in the settlement of Philadelphia we find recorded Cesar Ghliselin, a Huguenot, "who early cast in his lot with William Penn's *Holy Experiment* by the banks of the Delaware."

The famous Pine Tree Shilling

Then, of course, there was John Hull, a Boston silversmith, who was chosen master of the mint which was set up in that city in 1652. He it was who made the famous pine tree shilling. We are all familiar, of course, with the attractive arrangement he made with the Commonwealth, whereby for his labors in minting the coins of the realm he was authorized to keep for himself one shilling out of every twenty coined, an arrangement which enabled him to give as a dowry to his daughter at her marriage a pile of shillings that literally was her weight in silver. Other

Early Colonial Fork and Spoon attributed to John Coney

11

names familiar to collectors of early American silver are the New England silversmiths, Sanderson, Coney, Hurd, Burt, Dummer and the Moultons. Among the prominent New York craftsmen were Ten Eyck, Le Roux, Hastier, Goelet and Huertin; in Virginia—Kerr, Coke and Waddill.

Tea Pot by
John Coney
1655—1722

Our early settlers were men of vision. Many were merchants and traders. They built ships and traded to the far corners of the earth . . . around "The Horn" . . . for leathers and furs, to the Far East for spices and tea, to the West Indies for molasses to make rum which, with dried fish, they shipped to the Baltic countries and traded for sail cloth and rope, products we were then unable to produce. Through this trading, wealth accrued in our coast cities, and with wealth came the inevitable desire for better homes. In Virginia and other parts of the South beautiful mansions were built, while in New England, under the guidance of such immortal architects as Bulfinch and McIntire, there were created the countless now famous houses that stand to-day as model examples of Colonial design.

Colonial Spoons
c.1730—c.1765

In the beautiful homes of these successful planters and merchants we found silver and furniture in the same good taste. American craftsmen were quite the equal of their British cousins in workmanship and design, and while the importations from abroad were freely copied and established style trends, nevertheless, our Colonial silversmiths injected their own personality into their work and produced pieces of unusual charm and beauty. The early settlers, we will remember, were relatively limited in the number and variety of the tools with which they had to work, and from this as one natural cause, flowed the "simplicity" that characterizes the art of the period.

It was during this stage of "Colonial life in the manner grand" (1750-1812) that Paul Revere, the famous patriot and his father and his son were making their lovely pieces of silver tableware. Indeed, Revere's companion on the "Midnight Ride," William Dawes, was also a silversmith. Fortunate are those who have inherited down through their families a piece of silver of this particular period, not only because of its own intrinsic beauty, but because of the wealth of historic interest that attaches to it. We see here another reason why Early American silver is so rich in historical lore, for silversmiths of those days so frequently played leading roles in the affairs of Church and State.

While for the most part the few remaining pieces of Colonial silver are captive in the treasure collections of the leading museums, we can to-day enjoy the charm and beauty of these styles in the Colonial inspired designs and authentic reproductions which the members of the STERLING SILVERSMITHS GUILD make available through our leading jewelers.

Colonial Spoons
c.1765—c.1800

Probably no craft in America to-day is so rich in tradition or has such a well preserved heritage of its trade as the craft of the silversmith. Undoubtedly, the reason for this is that fine silversmithing is as much an art as it is a trade, and, regardless of mechanical advancement, a piece of finely wrought silver must *always* be the work of master craftsmen.

Good silversmithing is a trade that cannot be learned in a year or two. In Colonial times a boy frequently began his apprenticeship at the age of twelve. He actually lived with his master. Fashioning the precious metal became part of his daily life, and seven years was the commonly recognized period required for his complete training.

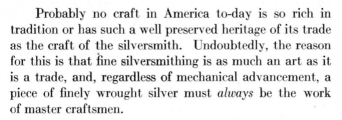

Tea Pot by Ten
Eyck circa 1730

While to-day the making of fine Sterling Tableware is more specialized in many steps of its production, and while modern methods have speeded its manufacture and accordingly reduced its cost to the consumer, nevertheless, as in centuries past, the maker must still have at his command not only the talent of trained artists, but smiths, die-cutters, chasers and engravers—each a master craftsman, each a student of design and deft in handicraft. The

13

old "Guild" note is apparent in a casual visit to the Silver-smith's plant of to-day, where we find as in days of old the various trades are frequently passed on from father to son.

Because the making of fine Sterling Tableware is such a highly skilled trade, and so closely knit from one generation to another, it is, after all, not surprising to find that its development has been practically confined to where first it was solidly planted, in Connecticut, Massachusetts, and Rhode Island. Here we find to-day the factors that give us silverware as beautiful as the world has ever produced for they have a heritage of fine craftsmanship that dates back to Colonial times.

This group of present-day master silversmiths, proud of the fine traditions of their craft and desirous of protecting and furthering their high standards of craftsmanship, formed a guild in 1917, as did the English silversmiths of the 14th Century. It is known as "THE STERLING SILVER-SMITHS GUILD OF AMERICA." The following companies are members of this GUILD:

Porringer by
Benjamin Burt
(1729-1815)

Colonial Spoons
c.1800—c.1830

The Alvin Corporation	Providence, R. I.
The Gorham Company	Providence, R. I.
International Silver Co.	Meriden, Conn.
Lunt Silversmiths	Greenfield, Mass.
Reed & Barton	Taunton, Mass.
The Towle Silversmiths	Newburyport, Mass.
R. Wallace & Sons Mfg. Co.	Wallingford, Conn.

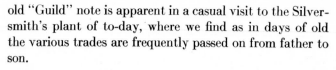

Tea Pot by
Burt—1765

Under the name of each GUILD member, listed on page 16 you will find that maker's own particular shop mark, or trade-mark. His trade-marks, or his name, the maker impresses on each piece of his product together

14

with the stamp "Sterling." These marks or names are registered and identify the works of master craftsmen. Solid Silver so stamped is your assurance of the quality of the metal, of the excellence of the design, and the reliability of its maker.

Leading jewelers of the country are the appointed distributors of GUILD Sterling. They will be found in every community and will take a genuine pride in pointing out to you the excellent weight, beautiful finish and fine construction of these products.

Colonial Tea Pot of the Type c.1765—c.1800

The extraordinary beauty and character of GUILD Sterling is self-apparent. No foreign made silver surpasses it in correctness of design or equals it in quality of workmanship.

Therefore, when you select your silver, you will want to look for the mark or name of a member of THE STERLING SILVERSMITHS GUILD OF AMERICA, and be assured of lasting satisfaction.

A large Silver Punch-bowl made by Paul Revere for the Sons of Liberty in Boston—1768.

15

IDENTIFYING MARKS

of

Members of the Sterling Silversmiths Guild of America

● THE ALVIN CORPORATION

ALVIN STERLING

● THE GORHAM COMPANY

GORHAM STERLING

● INTERNATIONAL SILVER COMPANY

● LUNT SILVERSMITHS

LUNT STERLING

● REED & BARTON

● THE TOWLE SILVERSMITHS

 STERLING TOWLE STERLING

● R. WALLACE & SONS MFG. CO.

  WALLACE

16

$\mathcal{F}ine$ $\mathcal{S}terling$...A WORK OF ART

Designing

Before the dawn of civilization everything was purely utilitarian . . . a dish was but a hollowed out gourd—a spoon was a shell set into a split-ended stick and tied tightly in place with thongs. These crude implements performed a necessary function, but . . . that was all.

As man became somewhat civilized he began to embellish his implements with crude carvings, and as he improved his implements he also gave more attention to their decoration. Nowhere is the development of civilization better recorded, or man's inherent love for beauty more clearly shown, than in the silverware of the ages. Always has this glorious metal been deemed worthy of employing the talents of the finest artist-craftsmen of each generation.

And so, to-day, it is only to be expected that among discerning women, *design* is of extreme importance when purchasing Sterling Silver Tableware. Since Sterling Tableware lasts a lifetime one wants to be sure that its design is not of transitory appeal, but instead, that it will always be in good taste—never out of style. It should be remembered, too, that the beauty of Sterling is as imperishable as the metal itself, and thoughtfully chosen, it will become the cherished possession of future generations.

How then can one recognize good design in table silver? First, look for good proportions and good contour. There are certain lines of harmony and symmetry that will be beautiful always. Even the untrained eye can sense this. Second, look for good balance—in well designed spoons, forks and knives good balance will be immediately "sensed" by taking the pieces in one's own hands.

The next thing you will consider in selecting your Sterling Silver Tableware is the design itself—and as previously stated, this is of extreme importance! Among lead-

Die-Cutting

17

Chasing

ing American silversmiths, design is given front rank in their own estimate of their product and their craft. To-day, here in our own country, there is produced among the member companies of the STERLING SILVERSMITHS GUILD, the finest fashioned silverware of all times . . . literally vying in beauty and craftsmanship with the works of Cellini, Platel and Paul Revere.

The creation of a well designed pattern is the work of an artist, frequently requiring months to develop. After the drawing has been perfected, it is modelled in wax (sculptured, so to speak) in order that the artist's idea can be fully and accurately set forth in the minutest detail for the craftsmen who are to produce it in metal. In the case of flatware, the design is then cut into steel dies for reproducing the many pieces of the pattern. The men who cut these dies are artists, thoroughly schooled in the fine arts, for the design in all its modelling must be carved intaglio in a solid block of steel. The hollow ware pieces are frequently decorated by hand chasing or hand engraving, crafts calling for the highest skill.

Just one word of caution in the selection of your pattern. Beware of low-priced Sterling and "Bargains." You will invariably find a reason for these baiting offers. In some cases the pattern is on the bargain counter because the design is inferior. In some cases it is because the pattern is a discontinued design or one the manufacturer is planning to discontinue immediately after the sale. In still other cases it is because the articles are poorly made. Remember, real artistry is never sold at bargain prices.

The opportunity of adding to your Sterling service is, of course, of prime importance. Naturally you want only a regular, (open stock) pattern which you can purchase year after year. Buy your Sterling from a reliable jeweler, for he will be as much concerned over your lasting satisfaction as you are, and gladly will extend to you a valuable service.

Engraving

Period Design

The term "period design" means a particular style of decorative art which predominated during some certain historical era. Most motifs of ornamentation are very old, and were originally inspired by plant or animal forms. These motifs have been used over and over again, redesigned or modified, to be sure, as the passing generations of various nations adapted them to their own particular taste or need. To-day, unless the object is entirely void of decoration, the type of ornamentation can usually be traced back to some historic motif. This is not simply characteristic of our own time, but true of all times.

Papyrus

The study of the many decorative styles is most fascinating. Covering as it does some 4,000 years, we will not attempt to treat fully such a lengthy subject in this small book. Nevertheless, we can give a brief outline of design which will be welcome. As we become more familiar with design motifs the greater is our appreciation of ornamentation and the greater is our enjoyment of the things we possess. Especially is this true of fine Sterling.

Lotus

Ornamentation has been defined as the manifestation of the thought and the imagination of what is beautiful. Man from the earliest time chose the object of his admiration and attempted to copy it or to adapt it to his own ideals of beauty . . . perhaps it was a flower, a leaf or a shell.

EGYPTIAN

At the right are decorative motifs used by the Egyptians 4,000 years ago. They are based on plants . . . the palm, lotus and papyrus. Other Egyptian motifs were the sun, beetle, animals and winged human figures.

Palm

GREEK

The ancient Greeks learned their art from the Egyptians. The acanthus leaf widely used by the Greeks can be traced back hundreds of years in Egyptian forms. The anthemion, or conventionalized honeysuckle, is a purely decorative Greek motif. Other characteristic Greek motifs of ornamentation were the laurel, the husk, the egg and dart, fluting, and the key or fret.

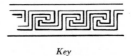

Key

Acanthus

Anthemion

ROMAN

The Romans conquered the world and in gathering great wealth took their art from the Greeks and brought it to a high state of development to satisfy the luxurious tastes of the time of the Caesars. This was the Classic Period to which designers have returned for inspiration time and time again during the past two thousand years. Below are the five Roman capitals known as the Five Orders of Classical Architecture.

Under Roman influence we find, in decoration, the use of festoons or garlands of fruit and foliage with animal forms and winged dolphins. This period also employed the acanthus leaf, anthemion, and other Greek motifs, but the feeling of the two styles is quite different. Greek art gives the impression of serenity and repose; Roman art displays power, exuberance, life, motion.

Ionic *Doric* *Corinthian* *Composite* *Tuscan*

GOTHIC

Gothic Arch

After the fall of Rome there followed the Gothic influence, 1100-1550. The style originated in northern France and spread throughout Europe. The characteristic motifs were the trefoil, quatrefoil arches, conventionalized oak and ivy leaves, and pointed arch. During this period most of the world was occupied in fighting. It was principally the church that had time, security, and

Gothic Floral Motif

money enough for learning and the finer things of life. It is not surprising then that the main impression of art during this time was ecclesiastical and was exemplified largely in architecture.

ITALIAN RENAISSANCE
1443-1564

The term Renaissance means re-birth, and as early as 1300 there was in Italy a reversion to the classic styles. Here commenced the real awakening of art and literature. This period gave the world such artists as Rafael, Michael Angelo and Benvenuto Cellini. Greek and Roman motifs were born again and worked into new fantastic patterns with masks, figures, birds and animals.

Mask Motif

21

FRENCH RENAISSANCE
1515-1643

Francis I influence

Francis I of France on a visit to Italy became imbued with the beauties of its works and returned with Italian artists and artisans to establish at his court this new style in buildings, furniture, tapestries and silverware. This style, as time went on, became more refined and truer to the Classic. Popular motifs were the acanthus leaf, fruit, husks, festoons, pendants, shells and scrolls. The Renaissance movement also spread to the Netherlands, England, Germany, Spain and throughout Europe.

LOUIS XIV
1643-1715

Louis XIV influence

Worthy of special note are the French styles between 1643 and 1793. Under the reign of Louis XIV decorative art assumed unequalled magnificence. The King established royal workshops and the best of the world's craftsmen were employed . . . no thought was given to time or expense. This era of glorious art continued through the reigns of Louis XV and Louis XVI.

LOUIS XV
1715-1774

Rococo

The style of Louis XV (1715-1774) is frequently referred to as Rococo. It was an exceedingly free style seeming to have no base, root or symmetry, yet carrying a certain balance and distinctive beauty.

LOUIS XVI
1774-1793

During the reign of Louis XVI, designers and craftsmen were profoundly influenced by the many classic treasures which had been unearthed in the buried city of Pompeii, near Naples, Italy. French decoration became more refined, detail more minute, lines more graceful. The style which developed spread throughout Europe and is plainly evident in the English styles of the Adam Brothers, Sheraton and Hepplewhite, whose works in turn influenced the design of our own Colonial architecture, furniture and silver.

*Louis XV
influence*

*Louis XVI
influence*

The characteristic motifs employed were slender acanthus leaves, garlands, baskets of flowers, urns, pendants, husks, rope carvings, festoons and ribbons. No period of ornament has provided designers with such an abundant source of inspiration.

*Louis XVI
Candle Bracket*

DIRECTOIRE AND EMPIRE
1793-1830

DIRECTOIRE was a simplification of the Louis XVI style more like the Grecian classic designs. Its leading exponent was Jacques Louis David, painter to King Louis XVI. The Directoire influence in America was most notable in the works of the famous Colonial furniture maker, Duncan Phyfe.

EMPIRE — Napoleon, when he became Emperor of France (1804), was determined to have an entirely new style of decoration. Following his campaigns into Italy and Egypt, he became imbued with Roman and Egyptian styles. Wreaths, laurel branches, the horn of plenty, winged figures, the sphinx, lions, eagles and arrows were typical innovations. Furniture was more heavily carved and silverware more massive.

ENGLISH RENAISSANCE
1558-1688

The foregoing pages have traced the development of design from Egypt to Greece, through Italy to France. During the sixteenth century France became the art center of the world, but other countries, in following the French, developed their own interpretations. It will prove of interest to trace a brief outline of some of the more important English styles for these were followed in early America and, consequently, have become part of our own present-day surroundings.

 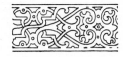

Bulbous Carving *Strap Work* *Jacobean Chair Back*
Elizabethan Motifs

It was during the reign of Queen Elizabeth (1558-1603) that the Renaissance showed its influence in England. Then came the Jacobean style (1603-1688). Both periods drew liberally from the Flemish and Dutch, as well as from the French, and the styles tended to become cumbersome and heavy, like the preceding Gothic.

Shell *Swag*

England's highest perfection in Renaissance design was reached between 1660 and 1685 during the reign of Charles II. The great designers of the period were Sir Christopher Wren and Grinling Gibbons. The style was much like the late French Renaissance, elaborate with pendants and festoons of fruit and flowers, shells, cupid faces, foliage and birds, but details and compositions were heavier—characteristic of the English.

WILLIAM AND MARY
1688-1702

James II, who succeeded Charles II, was so unpopular he was forced to flee the country. His daughter, Mary, who had married William of Orange, was called to the throne. They brought with them designers and craftsmen from Holland. Furniture, furnishings and silver took on simplicity and grace—a marked departure from the cumbersome furniture and over-loaded decoration of the preceding period. One of the most characteristic features of the style was the cyma curves combined with the half circle, used on chair tops, mirror frames, and in paneling of cabinets. It was at this time that tall clocks appeared, and they were exquisitely decorated with marquetry.

Chair Back

Marquetry Design

Cyma Curves

QUEEN ANNE
1702-1714

This style is deserving of mention because it is so frequently used by our present-day furniture and silverware designers. In furniture the characteristic features are the cabriole leg, the ball and claw and pad foot on chairs and tables. Through this period, surfaces, for the most part, were left plain. Such ornamentation as was applied was simple and confined largely to the familiar cockleshell.

Chair Back

Cabriole Leg

Claw and Ball

Cockleshell

GEORGIAN
1714-1820

Chippendale influence

Early in the reign of the Georges, Chinese importations had their influence on English decoration as noted in furniture of Chippendale, but the period as a whole was predominantly influenced by the contemporary styles of Louis XIV and Louis XV of France. The principal English designers besides Chippendale, were Hepplewhite, Adam Brothers and Sheraton. In the works of these artists you will find used the same classical motifs such as the acanthus leaf, swags, shells, scrolls, urns, rosettes, flowers and husks. Each of these Georgian designers, however, developed an individual style, and so strong, widespread and enduring was the influence of each, that

Hepplewhite influence

Sheraton influence

Chippendale

Hepplewhite

Adam

Sheraton

their styles are known by their various names. Above are sketched chair backs characteristic of each of these famous designers.

Previously, in speaking of the Louis XVI style, we commented on the influence this had on the Adam Brothers. Indeed, their inspiration came from the beautiful classic art uncovered at Pompeii. Their work is of special interest to us since they, probably more than any other designers, provided the inspiration for the best work of our own Colonial craftsmen.

Adam influence

Adam influence

It was from this style that Paul Revere drew much of his inspiration for his hollow ware. And designers of modern hollow ware, and flatware as well, find in this a type of decoration well suited to present-day tastes.

The work of the Adam Brothers introduced a daintiness and delicacy of ornamentation in marked contrast to the previous styles of early England. Their furniture was slender, refined and straight-lined. Surfaces were flat,

Typical Adam Motifs

embellished with the characteristic classic motifs, and especially popular with them were the griffin, urn and oval shield above illustrated.

   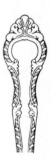

Medallion and Rosette   *Gadroon Border*   *Shell Motif*

While the spoons and forks of the Georgian period were very plain and relied almost entirely on engraving for decoration, the hollow ware was richly embellished

Examples of modern patterns featuring Georgian Motifs

with shells, scrolls and the distinctive Gadroon border. To-day GUILD silversmiths provide the flatware as well as the hollow ware in this very beautiful style.

American Colonial

Colonial, as a term, has come to mean a period of some two hundred years, from the landing of the Pilgrims in 1620 up to 1825. As the early American craftsmen followed the European, the styles we have previously described ran concurrently in this country. Particularly was this true of the English styles, up until the time of the Declaration of Independence, and then there was a decided swing over to the French.

Therefore, we see the same decorative motifs of the Jacobean, William and Mary, Queen Anne, Georgian, French Directoire and Empire, in so-called Colonial design. As previously mentioned in regard to silverware, there was in furniture and architecture a distinctly American rendition given to each style, and out of our Colonial period there have evolved many motifs which are recognized today as truly characteristic, such as the "bonnet" top—used over doorways, on top of secretaries, bookcases,

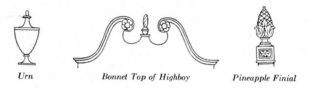

Urn   *Bonnet Top of Highboy*   *Pineapple Finial*

highboys and clocks—the American eagle, fan, shell, pineapples, festoons, husks, rosettes and reeding of the classic type.

Urn Motif   *Bonnet Top Motif*   *Finial Motif*

Above are sketched a few modern patterns, the designs of which have been inspired by typical Colonial motifs . . . the urn, the broken pediment or bonnet top, and the pineapple and acanthus finial.

VICTORIAN
1837-1901

The style Victorian, as the name implies, developed during the reign of Queen Victoria, in England, and ran concurrently in America. It comprised an individual interpretation of a number of preceding styles — Empire, Rococo, Jacobean, and Gothic. As interpreted in America . . . introducing naturalistic flowers and fruit ornamentation combined with graceful serpentine curves . . . the Victorian style has a certain, fanciful beauty all its own.

Examples of Victorian Furniture

The rosewood chairs carved in high relief in design of grapevines or roses, their backs slightly concave, and the well-proportioned mahogany sofas upholstered in rich damask or velvet bespeak the grace and elegance of that gay, romantic era.

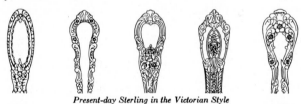

Present-day Sterling in the Victorian Style

CONTEMPORARY DESIGN

In addition to working in the traditional, period styles Guild silversmiths are constantly producing patterns in the Contemporary manner, creating entirely new and original patterns, yet adhering to the sound principles of good design.

Contemporary design is characterized by simplification, by fine structural form, and by the elimination of all but functional lines, curves and details. This influence

Examples of Contemporary Design in Flatware

is noted not only in modern architecture but in the designing of practically every form of useful or artistic article produced for the American home to-day.

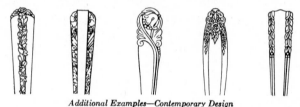

Additional Examples—Contemporary Design

Concerning American Contemporary art, the late Sir John Foster Frazer, English traveller and art critic, said, —"America is evolving and is developing that type of art that is neither Euranian, Mohammedan, Renaissance, or Allah knows what, but just American. I have seen and stayed in their wonderful houses that are an expression of the American temperament. I believe that in the heyday of American art, not only will it be as firm a type as Greece produced, but the houses will be more than living places. They will be typical of the people who live in them. Those who proclaim that the canons of art are defined for all time portray a lack of imagination. There is only one canon of art, and that is beauty."

Setting the Table

There is magic charm in the stateliness and sparkling beauty of a well-set table. Snowy linen, flickering candles, graceful flowers, fine china and crystal . . . all have a part in the lovely picture . . . but nothing is quite so important as the proud resplendent Sterling, and its correct arrangement.

The rules that govern table setting, like all good rules, are based on common sense and convenience. All forks go to the left (with the single exception of the oyster or cocktail fork), and spoons and knives go to the right, each piece being placed in the order of its use, from the outside in.

It is considered better form to have no more than three pieces of silver on either side of the place plate, unless the fourth is the oyster fork which is placed at the right of the plate, on the outside, alongside of the soup spoon.

Knives are placed so that the cutting edge is towards the plate. Butter spreaders are placed diagonally across the bread and butter plate on the upper right-hand side.

The glass is placed to the right near the point of the knife. When using more than one glass, arrange them at an angle.

The pieces of silver required at any meal depend on the menu. Therefore, accompanying the following pages which illustrate correct settings for the various occasions, we have listed opposite each page a simple menu to show its application.

The folded napkin is laid on the place plate, unless, for convenience, the first course is on the table when the guests are seated. The napkin is then placed to the left of the plate.

All flat silver should be evenly spaced on a line equally distant from the edge of the table.

BREAKFAST

MENU	FLAT SILVER REQUIRED
1. Grape Fruit	Grape Fruit (Orange) Spoons
2. Cereal	Dessert Spoons
3. Bacon and Eggs	*Dessert Forks and Dessert Knives
Rolls	Butter Spreaders
Coffee	Tea Spoons

ARRANGEMENT OF FLAT SILVER

LEFT OF PLATE—Dessert Fork.

RIGHT OF PLATE—Dessert Knife, Dessert Spoon, Orange Spoon. On the Bread and Butter Plate the Butter Spreader.

NOTE—The Tea Spoons for coffee are not placed at the individual place settings, but the Spoons are placed on the Saucer by the Coffee Cup and passed to the guests in this way after the hostess has poured the coffee.

TABLE COVERING

Bare table with mats is most popular and practical. However, an all-over table cloth may be used, in which case a cloth with color is preferable to a plain white one at breakfast.

NAPKINS

The breakfast napkin, like the luncheon napkin, should match the table linen. In the photograph it will be noted that the napkins have the same gayly colored floral pattern as the mats. Size of napkins illustrated is 17 inches square.

PLATES

Breakfast size, $8\frac{1}{2}$ to $9\frac{1}{2}$ inches.

TUMBLER OR GOBLET

At breakfast tumblers are to be preferred.

TABLE DECORATIONS

Centerpiece. Flower dishes, or compotiers of fruit.

The photograph shows the correct position of the large Coffee Pot, Sugar Bowl and Cream Pitcher, which are placed directly in front of the hostess. The Coffee Cups and Saucers with the Spoons on the Saucers are placed at the hostess' right. It is permissible to stack the Cups and Saucers if the table would appear crowded, as might be the case with a small table in serving six or more at breakfast. But whenever possible, as was the case in this instance, it looks very much better to have the Cups placed in their Saucers with the Tea Spoons in place on the Saucers.

*Most hostesses prefer this smaller size of Knife and Fork for use at breakfast. They are also called "Small Dinner" or "Luncheon" size.

LUNCHEON

MENU	FLAT SILVER REQUIRED
1. Oysters	Oyster Forks
2. Bouillon	Bouillon Spoons
3. Meat and Vegetables . . .	*Luncheon Forks and Luncheon Knives
4. Salad	Salad Forks
5. Dessert	†Dessert Forks
6. Coffee	After-dinner Coffee Spoons

ARRANGEMENT OF FLAT SILVER

LEFT OF PLATE—Salad Fork (next to plate); next to the left, Luncheon Fork. RIGHT OF PLATE—Luncheon Knife; next to the right, Bouillon Spoon; and farthest to the right the Oyster Fork. On the Bread and Butter Plate, the Butter Spreader.

TABLE COVERING

The question as to whether the table should be covered with a cloth, doilies, or runner, is one of personal choice . . . all are correct for luncheon. If an all-over cloth is chosen, a silence pad should be used.

NAPKINS

The luncheon napkin should match the table linen and is smaller than the dinner napkin. The correct folding is shown in the illustration; the open side of the napkin pointing toward the guest. Size of the napkin illustrated, 18 inches square.

PLATES

The regular size service plate (10 inches diameter) is set at each place setting.

GOBLETS

The larger is for water. The smaller for a beverage.

TABLE DECORATIONS

Centerpiece—Sterling Flower Dish. The Sterling Compotiers, one at each end of the table, filled with candies, also add to the charm and beauty of this simple setting.

Finger Bowls . . . are placed on the serving table or buffet and are never placed on the table until after the guests have finished eating the food which requires their use.

*Luncheon Knives and Forks . . . these are also called "Dessert" or "Small Dinner" size.

†When we specified the Dessert Fork for the dessert course we had in mind a pastry dessert. If pudding were served a Tea Spoon would be called for.

The silver required for the dessert course is always brought in with the dessert on the dessert plate.

AFTERNOON TEA

TO BE SERVED	SILVER REQUIRED	
Hot Biscuits	Kettle	Tray
Assorted Sandwiches	Tea Pot	Tea Spoons
Fancy Cakes	Cream Pitcher	Sugar Tongs
Tea	Sugar Bowl	Lemon Fork
	*Waste	

ARRANGEMENT OF SILVER

The large Tray holding the Kettle, Tea Pot, Cream Pitcher, Sugar Bowl and Waste is placed directly in front of the hostess; the Kettle with the spout pointing towards the hostess, so that it may swing forward for pouring. The Tea Spoons are placed on the saucers with the cups.

TEA CLOTH

There is a wide latitude in the matter of tea cloths, from the elaborate lace cloth to the simple cloths in pastel shades. Illustrated is a shell pink cloth of handkerchief linen with insert of real lace.

NAPKINS

Small size (about 12 inches square), matching or harmonizing with the tea cloth.

PLATES

Tea size: 8 inches diameter.

*An important accessory in pouring tea. When second helpings are served the hostess rinses out the dregs with hot water from the swing kettle, pouring the residue into the Waste Bowl.

DINNER

MENU	FLAT SILVER REQUIRED
1. Soup	Soup Spoons
2. Fish	Luncheon Forks and Luncheon Knives
3. Meat and Vegetables . .	Dinner Knives and Dinner Forks
4. Salad	Salad Forks
5. Dessert	Dessert Forks and Dessert Spoons
6. After-dinner Coffee . .	After-dinner Coffee Spoons

ARRANGEMENT OF FLAT SILVER

LEFT OF PLATE—Next to plate, Salad Fork. To the left, in the center, the Dinner Fork. Next, on the outside, the Fish Fork.

RIGHT OF PLATE—Next to plate, Dinner Knife. Next to right, Fish Knife. On the outside, at right, the Soup Spoon.

TABLE CLOTH

At dinner, beautiful white damask is always correct, although to-day, ivory, silver grey or light beige are equally acceptable. Even fine damask in pastel shades is sometimes used for variety or atmosphere.

NAPKINS

Large size (19 inches square), to match the table cloth. The correct fold and placing for dinner are illustrated.

PLATES

Dinner size: approximately 10 inches diameter.

GOBLETS

The Goblet is placed at the point of the Dinner Knife.

TABLE DECORATIONS

Flowers and Candles and Compotiers of candy. Nothing is quite so elegant and in such good taste as a Sterling Silver Centerpiece and four Sterling Candlesticks, such as have been used in the dinner setting photographed. The Sterling Compotiers also add charm and an air of hospitality to the dinner table.

Buffet Supper

The buffet supper provides a most convenient and happy form of entertaining a number of guests. The table is covered with a coarse weave linen cloth. The napkins are placed in stacks at one or two corners of the table. The silver and china are arranged in tasteful groupings.

Sterling silver candelabra are most effective in such a setting. Covered silver dishes, silver platters and chafing dish, as well as the large Sterling Coffee Set and Tray, also contribute so much to the attractiveness of the table.

The main dishes, such as cold meats or poultry, are usually placed at either end of the table. Creamed mushrooms, hot vegetables, etc., should be in covered dishes. The lobster Newburg, or eggs can be prepared in the chafing dish. The salad, olives, pickles, jelly and even the dessert are generally all on the table at its initial setting.

The plates should be of ample size and placed in piles, about eight to one stack. The flat silver is laid out flat in some conventional form at convenient places . . . do not rack. The serving pieces should be arranged parallel to the serving dishes.

At informal gatherings the gentlemen serve the ladies and then themselves. The waitress brings in the additional food from the kitchen or pantry and removes the used dishes, never allowing the latter to accumulate. Glasses are on the serving table. If there is room in the dining room, two or three small tables should be available for the guests on which to place their dishes when they have finished eating the course.

This method of serving is particularly adaptable for such occasions as wedding breakfasts, large luncheons, wedding anniversaries, as well as after a dance or cards. It is, of course, understood that the guests are not seated, although at a bridal function it is appropriate to seat the bridal party, and the rest of the guests are served buffet style.

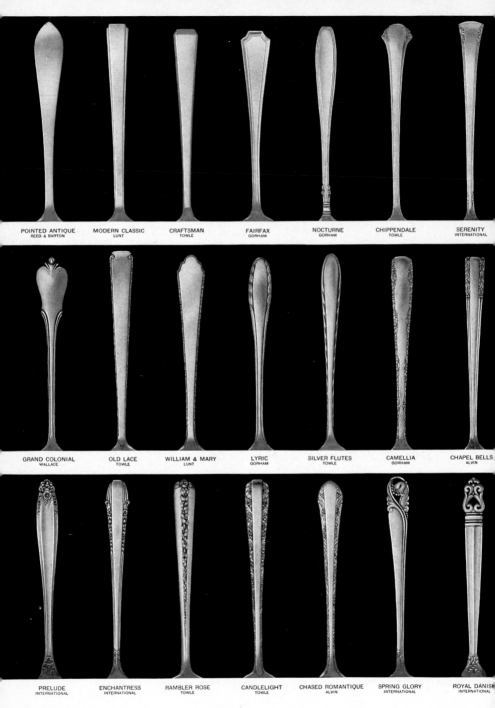

| POINTED ANTIQUE | MODERN CLASSIC | CRAFTSMAN | FAIRFAX | NOCTURNE | CHIPPENDALE | SERENITY |
| REED & BARTON | LUNT | TOWLE | GORHAM | GORHAM | TOWLE | INTERNATIONAL |

| GRAND COLONIAL | OLD LACE | WILLIAM & MARY | LYRIC | SILVER FLUTES | CAMELLIA | CHAPEL BELLS |
| WALLACE | TOWLE | LUNT | GORHAM | TOWLE | GORHAM | ALVIN |

| PRELUDE | ENCHANTRESS | RAMBLER ROSE | CANDLELIGHT | CHASED ROMANTIQUE | SPRING GLORY | ROYAL DANISH |
| INTERNATIONAL | INTERNATIONAL | TOWLE | TOWLE | ALVIN | INTERNATIONAL | INTERNATIONAL |

Here are a few examples of popular Guild patterns. They run the gamut from perfectly plain to elaborately decorated. That each one carries, even to the untrained eye, conviction of Correctness and Beauty, is no mere accident. Into their creation has been put a skill and

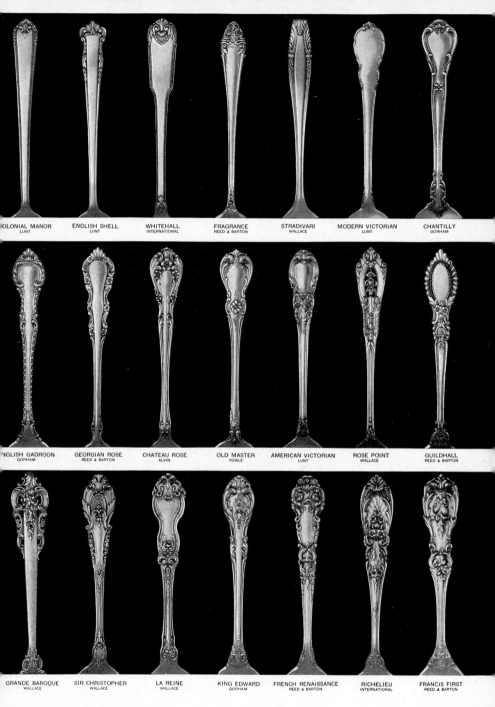

COLONIAL MANOR
LUNT

ENGLISH SHELL
LUNT

WHITEHALL
INTERNATIONAL

FRAGRANCE
REED & BARTON

STRADIVARI
WALLACE

MODERN VICTORIAN
LUNT

CHANTILLY
GORHAM

ENGLISH GADROON
GORHAM

GEORGIAN ROSE
REED & BARTON

CHATEAU ROSE
ALVIN

OLD MASTER
TOWLE

AMERICAN VICTORIAN
LUNT

ROSE POINT
WALLACE

GUILDHALL
REED & BARTON

GRANDE BAROQUE
WALLACE

SIR CHRISTOPHER
WALLACE

LA REINE
WALLACE

KING EDWARD
GORHAM

FRENCH RENAISSANCE
REED & BARTON

RICHELIEU
INTERNATIONAL

FRANCIS FIRST
REED & BARTON

craft of Artists that could be acquired only with long years of study and training. Students of Design will find it interesting to study these examples and note the ingenious skill with which the silver designer adapts traditional basic motifs to the peculiar requirements of his craft.

VARIOUS ITEMS

TABLE SPOON

DESSERT SPOON

TEA SPOON

COFFEE SPOON

ORANGE SPOON

BOUILLON SPOON

CREAM SOUP SPOON

SOUP SPOON

SALT SPOON IND.

SALT SPOON SERVING

OYSTER FORK

SUGAR SPOON

BUTTER PICK

SUGAR TONGS

SALAD FORK IND.

FISH FORK

DESSERT FORK

DINNER FORK

BUTTER KNIFE

ICED TEA SPOON

LEMON FORK

JELLY SERVER

ICE CREAM FORK

BABY FORK

BABY KNIFE

BABY SPOON

DINNER KNIFE

DESSERT KNIFE

FISH KNIFE

TEA KNIFE

FRUIT KNIFE

BUTTER SPREADER H. H.

BUTTER SPREADER FLAT

CHILD'S FORK

CHILD'S KNIFE

CHILD'S SPOON

in FLAT SILVER

ALAD or BERRY SPOON, SERVING

SALAD FORK
SERVING

PRESERVE
SPOON

COLD MEAT
FORK

EGG SERVER

CAKE SERVER

CHEESE
SERVER

PIE SERVER
WIDE BLADE

OLIVE FORK

OLIVE
SPOON

CUCUMBER
SERVER

TOMATO
SERVER

BON BON
SPOON

CREAM OR
MAYONNAISE
LADLE

GRAVY
LADLE

GAME SHEARS

STEAK KNIFE

STEAK STEEL

STEAK
FORK

GAME KNIFE

GAME FORK

MEAT KNIFE

MEAT FORK

MEAT STEEL

Silver Metal

History places the first sizable silver mines around the Mediterranean Sea. One of the oldest known mines was that of the Greeks in the town of Attica near Athens. Here to-day one may see the slag dumps from the mine worked more than two thousand years ago, where it is estimated that nearly a million ounces of silver a year

Silver King Mine near Park City, Utah

were obtained between the years 600 and 300 B. C. Later
... we read that the Romans worked the mines with
40,000 slaves in what is now Spain; and the Ancients
mined silver in the British Isles even before the Romans
came.

Silver has been found throughout the world, and its
story is written in the history of explorations and con-
quests of many lands. Twenty-six years after Columbus
discovered America, Cortez, Spanish adventurer, conquered Mexico and found cities rich with silver which the
Aztecs had been mining for centuries. For 300 years
while Spain ruled over Mexico, a steady stream of silver
flowed to the Mother Country. Even to-day Mexico is
one of the greatest sources of mined silver.

In the United States silver has been mined in quantity
in 18 states, but Utah, Montana, Idaho, Arizona, Colorado
and Nevada are outstanding as producers. Probably the
greatest single silver vein ever known is the Comstock
Lode of Nevada, discovered in 1858. This mine has yielded
as much as $6,000,000 worth of silver in a single month.

Of the world production of silver, about three-fourths
comes from North and South America. In 1946 the United
States produced 21.2 millions of fine ounces, Canada 13.9
millions, Mexico 46 millions; other Central and South
American countries 26 millions.

Silver is sometimes found free from other metals,
but usually it is compounded with lead, zinc, copper and
gold. To-day most silver is produced in conjunction with
the mining of these other metals. After the mined
ore is reduced to a metallic form by smelting, the pure
silver is separated by the electrolytic process of refining.
Then it is melted and cast into brick-shaped bars, known
as ingots, for convenient handling and shipping. These
ingots are then re-melted by the refiner, or silversmith,
to make Sterling.

⟨*Sterling*⟩ THE DECORATIVE METAL

We have confined our discussion largely to Sterling as the prized metal for use as Tableware. Sterling plays still another important role. It stands in a niche of its own as the regal, luxurious, mellowing medium of decoration. Place a Sterling vase in some drab or uninteresting corner in your hallway and note the difference. The Sterling Console Set makes the prosaic buffet a thing of beauty. The Sterling Centerpiece or Bowl of flowers or fruit lends charm and hospitality to the entire room. How the Sterling Tea Set takes your eye from all other decorations in the room, no matter how richly and tastefully furnished! — And on the dressing table, too! — Where is the substitute for Sterling? What else could speak so unostentatiously that note of propriety, of subdued richness, of beauty, of faultless taste? Truly, Sterling is the decorative metal!

What we have said bearing on the need for care in the selection of flatware design and decoration applies equally to our purchases of hollow ware. In this field, too, there is an added precaution we should take. Unscrupulous manufacturers will try to save this precious metal — skimp on it, we call it — in order to hold the lure of Sterling Silver before us — as a bargain. This they do by making their articles of a very thin gauge metal. True, what metal there is in these cheap products *is* Sterling Silver, but it is so thin, and there's so little of it that it can't possibly endure. It will bend and crack, and you will have a tawdry gimcrack — a cheap imposter. What one really buys in purchasing cheap candlesticks, for example, are cement or pitch candlesticks, thinly covered with a veneer of silver.

Study again the trade-marks and names of the Guild silversmiths reproduced on page 16 and look for them on the Sterling hollow ware and dresser silver you buy. Again, these marks, these names, are your protection.

The Simple Secret

OF KEEPING STERLING SILVER ALWAYS BEAUTIFUL

How to care for one's Sterling Silver Tableware could be covered well in one sentence. . . . *Use daily, at every meal, and wash thoroughly.*

When you hear a woman say, "I love my silver, but it is so hard to keep it clean," you are almost sure to find the trouble lies in the fact that she uses it only on special occasions.

Some hostesses cherish their Sterling so dearly that they keep it out of active usage, and therein lies the misconception. Sterling tableware of good weight, such as is made by the member companies of the Sterling Silversmiths Guild, can be used daily by one's family, and their children's children's family, without the least fear of wearing out. So its use and beauty should be enjoyed *every* day.

If you have seen the lovely pieces of antique silver in the museums, undoubtedly you marvelled at their wondrous beauty . . . their mellow finish, depth of color, their indescribable richness. This is due simply to usage . . . daily usage for generations.

Now it is true that this precious metal, if left uncared for, will tarnish. Rubber, Salt, Eggs (sulphur), gases and smoke are enemies of silver. But they will have little chance to affect your silver if it is used daily and washed thoroughly.

Anything which is so beautiful and so dearly cherished, you will agree is deserving of the same care and thought given fine linens, oriental rugs and choice china. So let us consider the few necessary, yet simple, things to do—and, not to do.

1. Use your Sterling Silver at every meal.

2. Rotate its usage. Bring all pieces into use during the week. For example, if you have eighteen Dinner Forks and, ordinarily, for your own family, use only six at a meal . . . don't use the same six all the time, alternate with the other two sets of sixes.

3. Next see that the silver is washed promptly after each meal. If salad dressing (containing sulphur in the eggs) is left on the forks, discoloration will set in, and salty foods might cause tarnish and black spots. Wash it in hot, soapy water. This is very important . . . *hot, soapy water!* See that all food, grease and other matter are removed. Next rinse thoroughly in very hot, clean water. Then dry immediately. Wipe thoroughly with a clean, soft cloth. Be sure that the pieces are *perfectly dry* before putting away.

Following the above simple rules will greatly retard tarnishing, but to enhance its beauty you will want to polish it occasionally—perhaps every month or so—with a good brand of silver polish. Rub each piece briskly *lengthwise*—never crosswise, or with a circular motion. After the surface has been brought to the desired color, wash thoroughly in hot, soapy water and rinse in clean, hot water.

If your silver is highly ornamented, clean out the silver polish which is likely to be left in the small crevices with a small brush. After the silver has been thoroughly cleaned, and dried, polish with a soft flannel or chamois.

As to chemical cleaning—by this it is meant, placing the silver in water in an aluminum container, adding salt and soda and boiling—this process does remove tarnish, but it also removes the "aging" tone or color of the metal, and therefore it is well to follow it up with polishing with a regular silver polish.

Now in regard to the scratching of silver: This is another bugaboo which often disturbs the hostess, especially during early usage when minute scratches are really unavoidable. As a matter of fact, these will add to the beauty of your silver, for millions of fine scratches will give the silver a more durable and practical finish than could ever be given mechanically. Therefore, the way to overcome the prominent appearance of the early fine scratches is simply to use the silver all you possibly can.

Of course, there are some pieces which, because of their very nature, do not come into everyday use, and these should be kept in tarnish preventive bags and rolls. Then there are tarnish preventive chests which are very practical if you should ever have to put away your flatware for any great length of time. All of these containers are available through your Jeweler.

Use your Sterling every day! . . . that is the simple secret.

With constant usage it will take on added color and beauty as the years go by. For, remember, the beauty of Sterling is "genuine" —in every piece the same precious metal extends all the way through. It is *solid silver*.

GLOSSARY

ALLOY
A metal resulting from the mixture of two or more metals.

APPLIED BORDER
A cast or rolled wire border or edge soldered on an article.

ASSAYING
The process of determining the fineness/or the constituents of a metal or alloy.

BRIGHT FINISH
The finish that imparts to Sterling ware a highly polished, mirror-like surface.

BUTLER FINISH
The care of silverware was one of the duties assigned to the English Butler. In the course of years of hand rubbing, the silverware took on a distinct lustre which to-day in modern Sterling ware is simulated by a process of manufacture known as "Butler Finish." This finish is sometimes called Grey Finish or French Grey Finish. Each may show a varying shade of *soft* finish, but both fall under the general category of butler finish as here described. The finish on Sterling ware is produced by buffing, or polishing the article with different kinds of abrasives. The various terms applied to soft finish are more particularly a trade convenience to indicate the abrasive used rather than to describe *standard* shades or tones.

CAST BORDER
An applied border made of cast silver.

CASTING
The process of pouring molten metal into molds and so reproducing the models from which the molds were made. These reproductions are called castings.

CHASING
Decoration done by hand with small tools and punches forced into the metal with tappings by a hammer. When flowers, scrolls, etc., are simply impressed into flat surfaces it is called *Flat Chasing*. When the ornamentation is brought up in high relief by driving out the metal from the inside and then modelled back into detailed form it is called *Repoussé Chasing*.

COIN SILVER
Silver assaying 900 parts pure silver to every 1000 parts. U. S. coins are made of this quality which it will be noted is 25 points lower than the Sterling standard.

CUTLERY
Knives with a cutting edge, (e.g., dinner, dessert, carving knives.)

DESSERT KNIVES
The trade name for knives which correspond in size to the Dessert Fork. A better term would perhaps be "small dinner" or "luncheon" size.

DIE CUTTING OR SINKING
The process by which a design or pattern is cut out of a piece of steel to form a "die" from which a quantity of similar articles can be stamped out or impressed.

DINNER WARE
The general term applied to dishes, plates, bowls, pitchers, salt shakers, candlesticks, tea sets and other hollow articles, as distinguished from knives, forks, spoons, toiletware, etc. (See Hollow Ware.)

DUTCH SILVER	Silverware imported from Holland. Generally very decorative and cast of silver metal very much lower than the Sterling Standard.
ELECTRO-PLATING	This process was introduced about the year 1842 and is used in making silver plated wares. By this process a layer of silver is electrically deposited on a base metal. (See Silver Plate.)
EMBOSSING	The process of decorating by striking or impressing the metal into a die with force.
ENGINE TURNING	The process of decorating through means of a cutting tool controlled by a craftsman following the design which is applied to the silver from a master pattern or stencil. This type of decoration, generally speaking, is confined to toiletware and novelties.
ENGRAVING	A process of hand decoration produced by cutting into the surface of the metal with engraving tools.
ETCHING	A process of decoration produced by what might be properly called "chemical engraving." The silver is covered with a protecting coating through which the desired design is cut and the design is eaten into the silver by nitric acid.
FINE SILVER	The Element Silver—Pure Silver—1000 Fine.
FINISHING	The general term applied to the various processes of polishing silver.
FLAT CHASING	See Chasing.
FLATWARE OR FLAT SILVER	The trade name for Knives, Forks, Spoons, etc.
GERMAN SILVER	A term used some years ago as interchangeable with Nickel Silver. See Nickel Silver.
GILDING	The process of Electro-plating a layer of pure gold on another metal.
H. H.	Means Hollow Handle. Cutlery and many fancy pieces are made by attaching a Sterling handle to the blade, tines, etc. These handles are made of two hollow halves and soldered together.
HALL MARK	The official mark of the Goldsmith's Company or other assay office or "Hall" in England, stamped on articles of gold or silver to indicate their purity. In America the Hall Mark is the word "Sterling" accompanied by the name or mark of a reputable manufacturer.
HAMMERED SILVER	A form of decoration resulting from repeated taps on the surface of the metal with a light hammer.
HAND WROUGHT SILVER	An article shaped and decorated from a flat piece of silver by a craftsman using only hand tools and such other non-mechanical aids as facilitate the use and manipulation of such hand tools. In the production of much so-called "hand wrought" silver the identical mechanical processes used in the initial shaping of the article in the normal course of silverware production are followed—and in these cases the term "hand wrought" is incorrectly applied.

HOLLOW WARE	Sometimes spelled HOLLOWARE. See Dinner Ware.
INSULA-TORS	Heat resisting substances inserted between the handle and the body of such articles as kettles, tea pots, etc.
KNURLING	An ornament cut originally into steel rolls and then impressed from these rolls into the silver as borders on bowls, dishes, etc.
LAPPED BORDER	An article is said to have a rolled edge or lapped border when the metal has been rolled over the edge and spun under to give the effect of a rounded edge.
MIRROR FINISH	A term applied to highly polished stainless steel blades.
MOTIF	The dominant feature of a design.
MOUNTS	Small pieces of ornamental metal. These may be ornamented wires, casts or stamped silver soldered on the article as decorations.
NICKEL SILVER	Contains no silver at all. A composition of copper, nickel and zinc.
OXIDIZING	Method of accentuating and enhancing the beauty of ornament by the application of an oxide which darkens the metal wherever applied. Some methods of cleaning silver will remove this oxide.
PATINA	The finish or surface texture. As applied to silver it refers to the soft lustrous finish the metal acquires with years of usage.
PIERCING	A form of decoration produced by cutting away parts of the metal with cutting dies, punching tools, or in the case of hand piercing, with a thin steel blade with fine teeth.
RAW EDGE	Term applied to Hollow Ware pieces the edge of which has not been turned over or mounted with a border.
REPOUSSÉ	See Chasing.
ROLLED EDGE	See Lapped Border.
SAW PIERCE	See Piercing.
SHEFFIELD PLATE	The original substitute for Sterling Silver, now displaced by Silver Plate. It was made by fusing sheet silver onto copper, rolling and manufacturing into hollow ware. The discovery of the electrolytic process of depositing silver on a base metal made it possible to produce articles of similar quality to Sheffield at lower cost and so the Sheffield Plate process was virtually abandoned (circa 1840). To-day, most fine pieces of "Old Sheffield" are found in museums and private collections and virtually none of it is available in the commercial market. Much electro-plated ware is erroneously advertised or otherwise referred to as "Sheffield Plate." In the purchase of "Sheffield Plate," be sure of the reliability and integrity of your dealer.
SILVER PLATE	Articles made of a non-precious metal on which is deposited pure silver by the Electro-plating Process. (See Electro-plating.)

SILVER-SMITHING	General term applied to the various crafts involved in making articles of silver. With advancing specialization in the manufacture of Sterling ware, the term has narrowed down to cover specifically the crafts involved in shaping, fitting, and assembling the various parts of an article into a complete piece.
SPINNING	A method of forming or shaping pieces of silver hollow ware by revolving a flat disc of silver over a piece of wood or steel which has been made in the shape the silver is to assume. By means of a tool, the silver is spread over the rotating form, finally achieving the desired shape.
STAINLESS STEEL	An alloy composed mainly of steel, nickel, and chromium, having generally greater strength than ordinary steel and possessing unusually high resistance to corrosion, tarnish, or stain by air, water and most acids.
STERLING SILVER	The word "STERLING" is the best known and most respected marking in use to-day. Pure silver alone is too soft for everyday use. Copper is the metal commonly used to give "STERLING" its added stiffness and wearing qualities. STERLING is often referred to as solid silver. It is composed of 925 parts pure silver in every 1000—this proportion never varies—it is fixed by law.
TOILET WARE (Dresser Silver)	The general term applied to combs, brushes, mirrors, manicure sets, and other dresser and vanity accessories.
WHITE METAL	A mixture of tin, antimony and copper in varying proportions.